The Essentials

Your one-stop-shop for life improvement and success with women

BENJAMIN RITTER

Published by Simplify Health LLC
Chicago, Illinois

i

This book would not be possible if not for all of the support I received. I want to thank my parents for inspiring me when I was younger to develop passions and follow my dream (which is how I found my love for soccer and eventually nutrition, self-improvement, and pick-up). My sister, Rachel Ritter, and Auntie Laurie Vincent, for their editing and support at the drop of a hat. Shahin and James for always being there for that extra push. My thanks also extend to all of the people, too many to name, who influenced me over the years; I hope you realize that you are in my heart and mind at all times.

TABLE OF CONTENTS

INTRODUCTION 1

HOW TO USE 9

MASCULINE TRANSFORMATIONS 13

SITUATIONAL AND APPROACH

PREPARATION 47

APPROACH AND INTERACTION 69

FOLLOW-UP AND RELATIONSHIPS 117

CONCLUSION 153

GLOSSARY 157

Introduction

I recognized a problem with clients and the general public while coaching in the social dynamic/pick-up scene; people don't act.

Overwhelmingly, the outcome with people who make the effort to study social dynamics and pick-up material is that you hold back from actual application of the learned material.

In the moment, you invent excuses for not applying what you've learned (not fully grasping the concept, not remembering the material, information overload, etc.). I can relate to that; I've spent hours reading, posting on forums, listening, watching, discussing, and searching for the next best thing, instead of actually *doing*. There is no action, no application, no usage or development of that carefully studied knowledge, which is what develops real skill.

These excuses will leave you unable to act when you're out trying to meet someone. You'll become discouraged, mentally re-play every missed opportunity, and become distracted from approaching women or taking advantage of opportunities that are right in front of you.

All in all, you don't *do*.

In recognition of this, I structured *The Essentials* to provide a pocket-sized, travel-friendly, pointed, guide of topics and tips on self-improvement and social dynamics.

The Essentials covers all the main ideas and actions that you will need in order to focus and refocus, to develop, strengthen, and automate key skills and beliefs.

With *The Essentials,* there will be no more racing through multiple books to prepare for a night out. *The Essentials* cuts out the clutter and provides your one-stop-shop for life-improvement and success with women. They are all about doing and evolving. These essential skills have been critical to others' and my personal success with women, and most importantly, in life.

Short and to the Point

Read this

Meet more people

Have more sex

Improve yourself

How to Use
The Essentials

Take *The Essentials* with you everywhere. Write in the margins, circle, highlight, dog ear, and mark it up; make this book yours. Follow the lessons and keep notes. Then do it all over again. Once you feel confident that you don't need a refresher, practice applying the concepts without reference, but always keep *The Essentials* out in the open for when you *will* need it again. Never stop learning and improving.

Masculine
Transformations

Let go of your past and recreate your reality. Your reality is created by how you choose to interpret your experiences. Anger, regrets, self-criticism, and other internal emotions are under your control. Changing them is as simple as deciding to alter how you think.

Stop using external achievements for internal validation. Focus on developing *yourself* for true fulfillment and happiness.

Align your actions to match your values and work toward your goals. Actions in conflict with your values will drain your happiness and block you from achieving fulfillment.

Do not limit yourself. All limits are self-imposed. Shoot for the stars in every aspect of your life. Decide, and then remind yourself daily of what you want.

Minimize excuses. Excuses are just ways to make yourself feel better about missing out on life.

Break the rules. Take risks. Test everything. Push your boundaries. Constantly put yourself in uncomfortable situations.

Lead and be decisive in your decisions and interactions. This demonstrates confidence and masculinity.

Leading does not mean controlling or knowing the outcome, it means having confidence, being opinionated, and being adaptable, in situations and life.

Act, believe, and live like you are important. Your very existence is a testament to how lucky and significant you are.

Always be "on" in everything you do, personality and physical appearance (energy, attitude, clothes, grooming). You're always being judged.

Always be aware of your current state, mentally and physically. Understand the cause of your emotions and use that understanding to depersonalize, accept, analyze, and control those emotions, regardless of the situation or people involved.

Recognize if a gut reaction is *intuition*, information derived from conscious or subconscious cues in your environment, or *projection*, an impression about a situation or person based solely on your own beliefs.

Learning how to distinguish between the two is important in becoming self aware.

Be patient and prepared to take advantage of opportunities as you learn and grow through new experiences.

Visualize accomplishing your desires. Place reminders in areas you'll see throughout the day. Believing and striving for something takes you a step closer to it actually happening.

Do not overload yourself to the point of unhappiness and confusion. Multi-tasking has proven inefficient. Immerse yourself in one task, enjoy it, and only when it is complete, freely move on to something new.

Spend your energy wisely. Every phone call, text, or night out, every time you even think about someone, you are expending energy. Letting others, or yourself, drain your energy, can leave you feeling sick, tired, and unmotivated. Be especially wary if you feel this way around certain people. Your energy should be a gift.

Label yourself as the prize. Decide specifically, yes or no, if the people you meet complement your life. Decide early in an interaction who is worth your time and energy.

Surround yourself with success. You become a product of your environment.

Be receptive to feedback. This is essential to stepping out of your internal perspective and seeing yourself as others do. But a word of caution, your friends' feedback will reflect their insight and wisdom, but also their biases and personal issues.

Always be learning, reviewing, and evolving. Choose something to work on every day.

Use the Golden Rule as your code of conduct. Treat everyone the way you would like to be treated, with honesty, trust, and respect.

Bring out the best in others, by being positive, supportive, and caring.

Be interested in what others have to say. Discover something interesting about each person you meet; everyone has a story.

Do not make assumptions about people based on gender. Men and women share the same capabilities and desires, from independence, and manipulation, to infidelity.

Search for ways to network for others. Bring people together who can help each other.

Balance the social and independent aspects of your masculinity. Do not feel guilty taking time for yourself, but make sure you are also taking the time to fulfill the social (including sexual) parts of your masculinity.

Reinvigorate your sexuality by valuing and seeing the beauty in the feminine. Femininity complements masculinity, and the two together have infinite possibilities.

Learn how to sexually fulfill women and make it a priority. Study the topic in books, articles, mainstream magazines and online. Don't be shy about asking questions and pay attention to her individual needs.

Emit pure sexuality through every aspect of your persona, how you dress, how you walk, and especially how you interact with the opposite sex. Breathe it in and out, in every look and in every movement. Accept your sexuality and have absolutely no embarrassment about how you feel and what you enjoy.

Accept that sex is something you must have in your life and be secure, not needy, in your sexuality. Men who worry about the next time they will be *allowed* to have sex are sexually desperate. View sex as a shared pleasurable experience.

Confidence presented as superiority or arrogance is being a douche bag. Don't be a douche bag.

Wear a condom, especially if you're not ready to raise a child, and be conscious of sexually transmitted diseases. Practice safe sex; be responsible.

Throw out all of your unattractive underwear immediately. Stop saving clothes you don't wear. Donate or just get rid of it all. Dress better and you will feel better.

Clean your room or apartment. Dust and vacuum once a week, keep your sink clear of dishes, your bathroom clean and stocked, and your bed made. Clutter looks less like a mess if it's organized.

Get enough sleep, 6-7 hours each night. Make sure to take enough personal time to recharge.

Meditate. Learn to slow your regular breathing too. At least three times every day, stop and breathe deeply.

Eat with the goal of optimum nutrition. A basic diet with few preservatives, lean protein, and complex carbohydrates, such as fruits, vegetables, and whole grains, will change your life.

Take care of yourself and stay fit, mentally as well as physically. Get a library card. Read books, news articles, and blogs. Work out, but also find a fun, social, and physical activity you enjoy.

Situational and Approach Preparation

Be mindful of the personality and characteristics that you display. People will react to your personality and actions according to their expectations. For example, if you only convey sexuality, you may be treated as a one night stand, regardless of your actual interest.

Do not base your current actions on previously held negative beliefs or labels about yourself. Every time you meet someone new, you have a clean slate and can even reinvent yourself.

Prepare yourself for ignorance and defensiveness in response to your high energy and confident attitude. Staying consistent and laughing it off is the best response to maintain control of the interaction.

Know the underlying purpose in your actions. People will test to see if your persona is congruent with your intent. For example, the more confident you are in your sexuality, the more women will question and make you prove it.

Dealing with general fear:

- Accept your emotion as a positive instinctual response (fight, not flight).
- Define and deconstruct it by visualizing your fear and how you desire to react.
- Discuss with a mentor (an alternate perspective) potential fearful situations and what you actually have to fear.
- Test yourself in fearful situations and observe and analyze your feelings with your new perspective.

Dealing with approach anxiety:

- Reframe. Imagine the worst and best that can happen in a situation. Choose. The worst is never worth losing the best.
- Women who inspire anxiety in you are the ones that are worth your time. Don't settle for less.
- Approach anxiety in essence is attraction, a beautiful opportunity.

Create personalized and fun responses to standard questions (about school, work, hometown, etc.) people ask upon meeting.

Know the social scene. Always have in mind at least two upcoming events, at different dates and times, to which you can invite someone who interests you.

Dispel the myth that you can only meet women in a bar or club. Meeting women at night can require more energy, different techniques and strategies, and involve competition with more stimuli. Meeting women during the day requires less energy, allows you to be more direct, helps make stronger impressions, and makes your day time more fun and interesting.

Choose a venue that matches your energy level. Do not go to a venue if your mental or emotional state will not match (unless you're willing to put in the effort to fake it).

Know everything you can about where you are going:

- Research the venue or the event for free entry, specials, the DJ, the best time to get there, etc.
- Pay attention to specifics, bathroom locations, closest bar, most congested areas, where women congregate, and alternate venues nearby.

Frequent an establishment. Become a fun, polite, regular on a specific night (preferably an off night).

Figure out the social hierarchy of your environment to arrange connections to specific people. Who can you meet, who will then introduce you to other people in whom you may be interested?

Remember names. Using them, and reminding others of your name, will make you seem like a friend, and increase the comfort level of interactions.

Befriend venue staff. Utilize down time, such as while waiting or people-watching, to speak with doormen, waitstaff, bartenders, and managers.

Tip well, but not extravagantly, especially if you intend to become a regular. How you tip dictates how you are viewed and treated by the staff.

Act like an assistant manager, the perfect role to emulate. Assistant managers spend their nights enjoying the atmosphere, socializing, and drinking, while ensuring that everything is running smoothly.

Know how much alcohol you can drink and stay in control of your actions. Nothing is wrong with drinking, but getting drunk does not make you more attractive, and puts you at a disadvantage in most situations.

Compare which sexual opportunity is more appealing:

The Drunk Guy: Limited to drunks, a date (usually drunk), women with low self-esteem, needy, or desperate, or previous sexual partners.

The Sober Guy: Limitless possibilities, any women he chooses, her friends, venue staff (strippers, bartenders, waitresses), every woman the Drunk Guy could sleep with, and more.

Use the venue, and anything associated, to meet people. Games, such as beer pong, flippy cup, darts, and pool, are easy socializing tools.

Eventually, focus your approaches on people who will complement your life. For example, even with someone to whom you are incredibly attracted, you need to figure out who she really is to evaluate if she is worth your time.

Approach and
Interaction

Stop worrying about approaching. The interaction will either be an incredible moment, irrelevant, or an amazing journey.

Approach, approach, approach. Never hesitate. If you don't approach, all of this is pointless.

Do not initially limit the people you approach to only those based on attraction:

- Preselecting based on attraction can be an excuse to not approach.
- People will surprise you.
- Change your mentality from *picking up* to being a social person and building your network.

Act as if you're being evaluated at all times. Just because you are not speaking to people doesn't mean they aren't paying attention.

Stand tall and confident, as if there is a taunt string attached to the top of your head, pulling you up.

Be the king when you enter a room. Tell yourself that you are strong, confident and sexy. Your body automatically displays how you think and feel.

Be aware of your emotional state and thoughts, before and during an approach. Review your thoughts from the past few moments. Thoughts control your actions and behavior. Positive thoughts and images will affect your posture, tone, and expression, which will influence others and their subconscious reactions. For example, if you are nervous or anxious, people will instinctively feel uncomfortable.

Use your actions to alter others' feelings and moods. During inter-actions, convey and project positive, engaging emotions through story telling, gestures, and your overall energy level. Never be emotionally or physically static in an interaction. In social situations, people tend to match emotional states to those directed at them.

Gain control and attention by approaching an interaction at a higher energy level. This makes it easier to incite emotions in others.

Eye contact with a smile or a double-take is an opportunity to approach. Waiting creates awkwardness and shows weakness. Searching for eye contact however, can be perceived as desperate.

Approach women in a non-threat-ening manner at the beginning of the interaction. Stay in line of sight, and apply non-direct, non-confrontational body language.

Capture the attention and focus of a group or woman, before attempting a lengthy line or story. If no one is paying attention to you, they will not pay attention to what you are saying.

Take advantage of pre-openers offered by your surrounding environment; they are natural opportunities for starting conversation.

Create three conversation starters relevant to your life which you can use to begin and continue an approach.

Don't be every guy. Most men approach, discuss, and answer questions in the same way. It's like a broken record. Make your conversation interesting and emotive by using memories as examples and speaking as if you are telling a story.

Answer questions indirectly and in a non-conventional way. Avoid asking yes or no questions, instead use open-ended questions. These are tools that will naturally lead conversation to new topics and stories.

Pause. Take your time and do not rush an interaction. Silence is powerful, and, if used properly, can be a strong indicator of status and confidence.

Always speak from your diaphragm and slower than may seem natural. Based on the emotion that you want to convey, vary the tone (inflections) and rate (speed) of your voice. Learn to understand the impressions caused by changes in your voice. Try recording your voice in different tones, deep, slow, and fast, while observing for how it makes you feel.

Commit completely to your movements. Do not hesitate. Move your hands, eyes, lips, and every other part of your body with confidence.

Always be positive, it breeds positivity. Cutting humor, playful negative body language, etc., in an interaction must be softened by a positive action, such as a smile or hug.

Imply in the beginning of an approach that you have somewhere else to be, so that others will not quickly try to end the interaction if it is uncomfortable. This gives you more time to build attraction in an interaction.

Incorporate touch. Physicality builds momentum in an interaction. Platonic and non-overt sexual use of physical contact will imply familiarity and breed sexuality. Touch helps build connection and demonstrates interest. For example, dance moves involving spinning, and even physical games, such as thumb wrestling.

Eye contact, 80 percent focused on and 20 percent off the person, is an indicator not only that you are listening, but also of interest and confidence.

Try to immediately gauge your target's confidence. A woman's self-esteem and confidence will alter how she reacts to your level of sexuality and confidence. More confident women are more likely to be open to cocky sarcastic banter, while those with less confidence may reject an approach that includes sarcasm or sexuality.

Focus on feelings and less on details (personal information) during your initial interactions. Most people you meet on any given night don't truly care about your past or who you are, they only care about how you make them feel.

Make assumptions, after you have gained some background information about a woman's desires, passions, and personality, in order to segue into topics that will be more meaningful for her.

Respectfully challenge and gauge, but always be mindful of other's limits.

Successful interactions can be based on a foundation of practiced skill sets, but each is unique and dependant on the other person's perception and specific situation. Adjust conversation topics, responses, and actions based on that perception.

Qualifying someone is when you challenge his or her attributes in a way that will cause a defensive response.

Qualifying is generally a good way to discretely gain investment. When someone is defending his or herself, they are trying to positively affect your opinion and gain your approval.

Liking someone is very different from sexual attraction. Focus on attraction. Attraction is a sexual emotion. When she is attracted to you, she is also interested in finding out more about you, and her expectations and thoughts of you will include sex.

Do not qualify, or show obvious signs of attraction or interest, until she has shown that she is attracted and interested first.

Gain approval from her friends. Pay attention to the social hierarchy of the group and focus your charm on the leader or protector. Be fun, positive, and non-threatening.

Try to spend time with her alone. Even with her friends' approval, the more people involved in an interaction, the more difficult it will become, and the less you will be in control.

Any interruption needs to be under your control, or you risk losing the entire interaction. If someone intrudes, maintain your dominance in the interaction. Attempt to be the focus of conversation or create a situation where the intruder appears boring, by introducing mundane topics into conversation.

There is almost no pick-up in which another guy, even a friend, can help. Most are pre-disposed to attempt to diminish your status during inter-actions. If you must interact with another guy, dominate the conver-sation, ask qualifying questions, be friendly, and maintain the conver-sation with the woman. Ask him about uninteresting topics, say you have to go, and take the woman away.

Always find out the logistics of your target and/or group. Time constraints, venue changes, and location affect every interaction. For example, if you want to go home with her, you may need to figure out how she got there, who she is with, her plans for the next day, where she stays, does it need to be overnight, does it need to be this night, or where else you can go, to keep the momentum of the interaction.

Forget about the phone number. A phone number has no commitment. Make plans with her first, and only then request the number to call for details.

People value what they have more once it's taken away. Make others feel that they lose something when you leave and gain something when you return. Use this to build attraction and momentum in an interaction. For example, after an extremely positive interaction, leave for a bit, or after touching her for a while, stop touching her.

Getting others to invest in you builds a stronger bond. Anytime others spend personal or intimate energy on you, such as doing you a favor, or especially, sleeping with you, they will look back and justify their actions by recalling stronger impressions of your worthiness. Most people will then reason that you must be worthy of that investment.

Always search for and instigate fun. For inspiration, think about children, who hate being bored and are able to find fun in the simplest activities through their high energy and wild imaginations.

Role play, telling a story by using something from the interaction to place those with you in fantasy roles (superhero, flight attendant, bad girl, etc.) creates momentum and sparks the imagination. If the response is positive, remember the character or event, so that you can use it in future interactions, to bring back the associated feelings of fun and familiarity.

In highly emotional states, our mind creates anchors to physical things. This is as simple as others wanting to see you because they have fun when you are around. Another anchor is responding sexually to those with whom we are regularly sexual. We have anchored those actions to that presence. The more exciting and emotional an interaction or event, the more positively others will view you and the relationship.

Make sure to smile and appear to be having fun in any photos. Photos supply no information other than body language to create a first impression and will be up on social media sites in no time.

When someone does not appear interested, pushing makes that person uncomfortable and makes you appear desperate. Build attraction by appearing uninterested in her disinterest, inciting jealously, connecting with her friends, and, if possible, leaving for a bit, on a positive note.

Smile at rejection. If someone "rejects" you, he or she most likely would not be a positive addition to your life. Be happy that person saved you the trouble of disqualifying him or herself.

Always be consistent throughout an interaction. Everything you say about yourself is now part of who you are.

Stay true to yourself. Get caught up during interactions, but make sure not to be persuaded by others' emotional states.

Take notes about the people you meet and your interactions, then review them in order to gain a better understanding of your experiences and other people.

Meet someone multiple times (pre- ferably in different settings) before forming conclusions and judgments. It takes time to develop a complete view of a person's character and personality.

Get out of your head and pay attention. Use information from the environment to understand the social dynamics of a situation and prepare for future interactions. For example, what can you read from her posture, expression, and even her friendships?

Clothes, body language, accessories, and specific terms in conversation all provide information about who she is and how she thinks.

Follow-up and Relationships

Decide and work towards the type of relationship you'd prefer (monogamous, polyamorous, open, closed, etc.). Never agree to or give the impression you desire a relationship that is outside your long-term comfort zone for short-term gains (such as sex or companionship).

Do not rush or be pressured into any relationship. Take your time to get to know the person and be sure it is what you want, before fully committing.

Maintain your identity when starting a relationship. For example, don't spend all your social time with her, because eventually you will want to spend time with your friends. If her previous expectations include devoting all your time to her, this could cause resentment.

Never base a relationship on a false identity.

If you feel guilty, you are probably being dishonest.

Different forms of communication, from email to texting, to calling and in-person, vary in intimacy and effectiveness toward furthering a relationship. For example, use texting to have fun and keep relationships current, but avoid telling long, drawn-out stories. Base your usage on what you want to accomplish.

Take advantage of opportunities, especially during the initial interaction. For example, when "friending" on Facebook, send a personal note. Instead of taking her number, add yours into her phone with a memorable moniker, and then call your own phone.

Do not use the same means of communication twice, and do not try to reach out through more than two means of communication before receiving a response.

Leaving a voicemail for someone you just met can be difficult. To increase your chance of getting a return call, refer to a previous experience, include gratification, be positive, and stimulate curiosity. For example, "Thanks for your advice the other night, it was amazing. Call me back so I can let you know what happened."

Do not respond to her faster than she responds to you, through text, email, or phone, at the beginning of your interactions.

Stop texting women that are unresponsive. Call or text her three times, and if she doesn't invest, delete her number.

Contact a person when you know he or she is alone or bored. Communication during this time has less competition and will have greater impact. For example, before she goes to bed, or when she visits family for a weekend.

Only pay for someone because they deserve it and if you want to, not because you feel obligated. As a general rule it's good to avoid expensive activities in the initial phase of the relationship.

Addressing canceled plans:

- Reframe your perspective and do not take it personally. How often do you change or cancel plans with friends?
- If it happens multiple times, directly inform her that if she wants to see you, she now has to make the effort.
- Attraction is not enough to guarantee plans. You cannot seem like a stranger. Preempt the possibility by building comfort, trust, and especially excitement about spending time with you.

Schedule other plans for after a date in order to give the evening a natural end and keep initial interactions short.

Going out together while being in a relationship can include:

Just the two of you: Take your time together. Interact with other people when appropriate, but your partner is always number one.

Your social group: Help your partner be OK with being second, by making sure she is getting the right amount of attention. Being social with strangers must be done delicately, but tends to be acceptable if you bring them into your social group to meet others.

Going out together while being in a relationship can include:

Her social group: Learn to be without her by your side. Befriend her friends and give her the space she needs. Reaching out to strangers must be done delicately, but will keep you entertained if she is occupied for a large portion of the night. Use this to show her that you are independent. Be careful to avoid stimulating her jealousy too much by simultaneously showing her attention, even though you will not be her main focus.

Going out together while being in a relationship can include:

Both social groups: This is the ideal situation. Introduce friends and help start conversations. Be the instigator. Every now and then, check on your partner. Reaching out to strangers and meeting new people should not be a focus. Again, you will not be the main focus of her attention.

Intimacy, expressions of familiarity and affection, is an important aspect of every type of relationship, even purely physical ones.

Loneliness can be prevalent no matter how many reliable, trustworthy people are around. Loneliness is a lack of intimacy. Invoke passion, care, and focus when creating a bond, to avoid loneliness and build intimacy.

Successful long term relationships include independence, attraction, intimacy, trust and commitment.

Be patient. Attraction and an intimate connection are meaningful, but do not symbolize actual commitment. Commitment does not develop without time and investment.

Remember why your past relationships were successful and unsuccessful. Learn from your mistakes.

Don't expect your overall impression of a relationship or person to change unless something is done to drastically alter your perception. This goes for first impressions, infatuations, and previous and current sexual or long term relationships.

Make the most of your time, in relationships and in life. Don't be afraid to kick someone out of your life who misuses and wastes your time.

Pick your battles when it comes to pushing arguments. Does it really matter?

Place yourself in your partner's shoes when evaluating an issue. Keep yourself emotionally level and fair when reacting.

Avoid needy and immature actions, such as accusations, anger displays, irrationally, and excessive attempts at communication, from yourself and in others.

If you think something is wrong, or there was an argument, and your partner said, "I'm/It's OK," offer comfort, but let her deal with it. Do not press the situation.

Take the time for a heated situation to settle before attempting mediation or resolution. Generally people are motivated and persuaded by the state or foremost emotion they are feeling in a moment. Logic-based arguments or persuasion are not the best use of your energy when emotions are running high.

Never speak negatively about her family or friends, while still supporting her emotional state (even if it's negative). Comfort and reassure her that what she feels is fine, but do not join in or criticize.

No one else cares about the success of your relationship. Be careful of other people's intentions. Base your relationship decisions on open and honest communication with your partner.

Warning signs that represent your partner is having doubts about your relationship:

- Disinterest in sex.
- More controlling behavior.
- Easily annoyed and frustrated.
- Distant and less frequent communication.

How to react if you want to revitalize your relationship:

- Focus more attention on your life and interests, to develop more of what attracted her to you in the first place.
- Reflect on your own inappropriate or weak actions in the relationship.
- Withdraw (call and see your partner less) to give her the chance to miss you.
- Be stronger in your decisions and limits, to display your independence and standards.

Never end an interaction or relationship on a needy or desperate note. Revealing all of your hidden emotions as a last-ditch effort to convince them to like you will not work and it will ruin future opportunities to redeem any semblance of a relationship.

A relationship cannot be stolen or taken. A person is not a possession. You cannot blame a person for finding someone else to provide what you are not in the relationship.

Sustaining a relationship requires:

- Awareness of the needs of your partner and your own.
- Addressing conflict and concerns without punishment or negativity.
- Open and honest communication.
- Shared and independent experiences.
- Compromise.

Conclusion

The Essentials is meant to connect, inspire, and positively influence the core values in your journey to become a greater man. Over the years, I have learned and taught that the most important values are to always be confident, but humble, treat everyone with respect, keep an open mind, find your passions, live true to yourself, take advantage of opportunities, realize that many of your worries are just blips in the overall journey of life, and that when in doubt, just say, "Hi."

Please email me with any questions or for further learning and mentoring.

Benjamin Ritter
TheEssentials@Benjamin-Ritter.com

Glossary

Approach Anxiety: Fear and stress from the opportunity or idea of approaching a person or group.

Calibrate: Gauging the personality and perceptions of those around you and adapting and altering your actions to display similarities.

Day Game: Applying pick-up skills during the day.

Logistics: All details, such as transportation, timing, and location, regarding the person or group in which you are interested.

Flaking: Showing disregard for and canceling plans.

Gut Reaction/Instinct: Perceived information based on a collection of conscious or subconscious cues from your environment.

Night Game: Applying pick-up skills during the evening.

Open: To start a conversation with an individual or group of people.

Opener: Anything that is used to open an interaction with an individual or group of people, such as a comment, story, physical signal, etc.

Pre-opener: Opportunities that lend themselves to an opener with a specific person or group. For example, a situation, article of clothing, spilled drink, coincidence, etc.

Projection: When you perceive something about a situation or person(s), based solely on your internal beliefs.

Qualify: When someone responds defensively about or denies characteristics about him or herself in order to improve your opinion of him or her.

Reframe: Altering your negative perspective of a situation into a positive. Also applies to deliberately reinterpreting or altering the meaning of a comment from someone during an interaction in order to create momentum.

State: Your emotional and physical self at any given time.

About the Author

Benjamin Ritter, MBA, MPH and Co-founder of Suave Lover International found his passion in social dynamics and personal development through the interest in the field of public health and the pursuit of a more exciting lifestyle. Years of mentorship, academia, professional experience, and dedication to self-development have made him into the professional coach and writer he is today.

Sports, fitness, nutrition, social dynamics, and public health are his focus areas. These interests fuel his passion to guide and provide tools for men to learn and regain the lost, albeit natural, art of attraction.

Made in the USA
Middletown, DE
26 September 2019